GREATER VANCOUVER

Touch the magic

British Columbia, Canada

A Photographic Essay by
PHILIP HERSEE

Foreword
RAYMOND BURR

Introduction and Word Imagery
KEN BUDD

Graphic Design and Art Direction
ALEX GREEN

Finished Art Assembly
KITTI TOUZEAU & ALEX GREEN

Twilight diamonds crown snow-kissed peaks. **(West End, Vancouver)**

GREATER
VANCOUVER
Touch the magic

by PHILIP HERSEE

ACKNOWLEDGEMENTS

There are always those without whose help the creation of a major work would not be possible. To those named here, and to the many others who allowed us to touch their magic, we extend our deepest appreciation.

- Alex Green and Kitti Touzeau of Alex Studio Limited
- Larry Lunn and Gord MacDougall of Connor, Clark and Lunn Investment Management
- Mr. Raymond Burr
- Michael Burch of Whitecap Books Ltd.
- John Dunkley and David Honey of Key Colour Photo Lab Ltd.
- Kevin Miller and Cameron Young
- Jeff Morgan and Adam Lewis, our 'Men in the Country'
- Joan Hall, Jean Gelwicks, and, Steve and Andy MacDonald
- Jacqui, Shannon and Bill Oldham of Lanzarac Acres
- Brian Croston, and Doug Cameron of Emerald Sea Photo Ltd.
- Brett Peters and Greg Kocher of The Diving Locker
- Steve Wright and Vancouver Helicopters Ltd.
- Melissa Wolf and International Artists Ltd.

- *John Bartosik, photographer and author of 'Sea To Sky Country'*
- *Bob Faulkner and Agency Press*
- *Zenith Graphics Ltd. and North-West Bindery Ltd.*
- *Al Fedyna, and, Joe Schofield and Cory Maedel of Apex Ultralight Flight Centre*
- *Sue and George Mills of Southland Riding Village and 'Arden's Heir'*
- *Grouse Mountain Resorts and the Hang Gliding Team*
- *The Chilliwack Rhythm Reelers, and Clyde Dougans*
- *Gerry O'Neil and AAA Horse and Carriage Ltd.*
- *The Museum of Man, University of British Columbia*
- *Florohn Photographic Ltd.*
- *Les Richards for his technical assistance*
- *Anne Pobst for her editorial assistance*
- *The helpful and courteous Staff of the Vancouver Public Library*
- *Celia Duthie and Sam Fogel and*
- *Nigel Marsh and Wayne Cousins*

DEDICATIONS

To my wife **HILDA** *and son* **DUSTIN,**
my family in Canada, and,
to my parents and family in England.

Phil

To **GORD,** *my mentor,*
JEFF, *my friend,*
and,
MOM, NAN, BONNIE, BETTE, *and* **JEAN,**
the special ladies in my life.

Ken

TABLE OF CONTENTS

FOREWORD

When I was a small boy growing up in Canada, we used to say laughingly, to be sure: "Vancouver?...oh, it's just outside New Westminster!" In the half-century or so since those carefree days, I have grown up—a lot!

Vancouver was always a jewel of a city, of course; now it has reached out to embrace the elegance of modernity and technology with the same fervor that it sheltered and sustained the classic qualities of the great metropolitan centers of the world.

Vancouver has always welcomed diversity—in culture, in lifestyle and in philosophy—and woven these bright threads into its handsome fabric. But as the adage has it: "the more things change, the more they stay the same." Vancouver—taller, bigger, busier—adhering to a set of civic standards as constant as its signature gardens, is still the many-faceted city of my youth...

I have always held, as an article of faith, that there was no way to capture exactly and reproduce the very essence of a city. It may be that Philip Hersee and Ken Budd have done just that; their beautiful book does indeed, 'touch the magic'!

Vancouver, Greater Vancouver! certainly one of the Almighty's most glorious creations; nurtured by—and for—Canadians, all Canadians. Created and nurtured to welcome their friends... All their friends!

Raymond Burr

RAYMOND BURR

INTRODUCTION

It is Canada's gateway to the Pacific Rim, and rich in ethnic diversity. While young by historical standards, the Greater Vancouver area is already touted as one of the most beautiful places in the world. The people like it because the seasons are varied enough, the environment is certainly magnificent, and a multitude of experiences are ever-waiting.

The sun threatened to abandon the day, leaving a wash of gold over English Bay. The sand still held heat, encouraging 'Sun Gods' to linger. Human seals cavorted offshore.

Couples of all persuasions wandered the Sea Wall. An elderly twosome walked quietly side by side, their pace quickened by the Cocker Spaniel tugging at the end of the leash held by the grey-haired woman. A group of young men joked its way along, eyes casting in all directions, seeking out new companions. Lovers made a fluid gait from entangled limbs.

Windsurfers dodged swimmers the way bicyclists avoided walkers.

The runner contained his urge to break immediately into stride. Tendons and fibres protested their awakening as he methodically worked through each stretching exercise. Frustrated by the barrier of bodies ahead of him, he began his run.

Picking his way among the ramblers, he wished for his own highway of clouds. The odours of the evening assailed his senses, and he became enthralled by the pungent perfumes, coconut oil on a sunbather, smoke from a different cigarette, and the aroma of fresh popcorn.

People shared their smiles, and he reciprocated. The rhythm of running came easily as fire spread across the ocean.

It was summer in Greater Vancouver.

The clear, green water gurgled as the paddle slipped through it. A slight current carried the canoe along the Serpentine River, making the action of stroking almost effortless.

The man smiled down at his son and daughter snuggled in flotation jackets and fast asleep on the bottom of the craft. Their mother sat at the bow, her paddle idle across the thwart. She breathed the crisp air deeply, and pondered whether the 'Indian Summer' sun was warm enough to warrant removing her bulky sweater.

They had been on the river for a couple of hours. Drifting first by a golf course, the young children had been amused by the clicking sound made when the ball was struck. They were equally fascinated by the unique 'fishing pole' two teenage boys used to raise the small white spheres from the shallows.

Other fishing rods dangled over the water as well. Fishermen, pleasured by the serenity of the day, relaxed in lawn chairs while their baited hooks tempted coho salmon and cutthroat trout.

All four had scrunched up their noses as the acrid smell of a poultry or fur farm wafted past. The spreading of manure on a field occasionally added to the pungency.

Although it was Sunday, a full measure of activity was apparent at the numerous market gardens. Crops of cauliflower and cabbages were still being picked. An early frost encouraged the harvesting of parsnips, and pumpkins sat begging to be carved.

In addition to making several stops to peer over the dike, they had picnicked on a grassy bank next to an acreage with a paddock beside a small barn. A little girl was training her pinto pony, and the daughter had whined that she wanted one just like it. Oatmeal and raisin cookies had distracted her.

Shortly they would reach the Serpentine Fenn Bird Sanctuary where they would be met by the children's grandparents. The older couple often wandered among the marshes, listening for the honks from Canada geese or whistles from widgeons. They particularly enjoyed th antics of the blue-billed Ruddy duck.

A light breeze carried the drone of an ultralight flying overhead, and rustled the golden leaves of a poplar tree silhouetted against the vivid, blue sky. Somewhere ahea a cock pheasant crowed. They were nearing the Fenn.

It was autumn in Greater Vancouver.

Soggy clouds hung over the valleys and congested inlets, but atop Grouse Mountain the impressive vista overlooking the city and outlying communities remained unobstructed.

Skiers waited their turn to sit the lifts that would carry them even higher to snowy thresholds. Quilted warm-ups, jeans and stretch pants snugged buttocks, while jackets and sweaters of the most vibrant colors protected torsos. Toques and headbands were more symbols of the activity than dictates of the weather. There were no ski-masks to filter the clean air.

On the Peak, two teenagers surveyed their chosen courses, adjusted goggles, and started down.

Her route was near to the trees where powder crystals and feathers of ice offered a blanket of softness. She sat back on her skiis and let gravity do the work. Shifting her weight and twisting her body almost imperceptibly, she created a perfect ride.

He carved tracks identical to those of someone before him around the first few moguls. He picked up speed, the cold air injecting him with exhilaration. He changed his course and aimed straight down the fall-line, his body bucking and reeling as he bashed off the crests of successive humps.

Catching an edge, skiis and limbs became a tangle of color and white. He careened and buffeted to a sliding stop. He lay still for a moment, expecting pain to invade his being. None came.

Two young girls, friends of the mountain, laughed and sent sprays of snow over him as they scooted past.

It was winter in Greater Vancouver.

It was an extremely active group of senior citizens. In the past month, the fifteen of them had been enamoured by the paintings of Emily Carr at the Vancouver Art Gallery, had listened to a thoroughly entertaining and educational lecture as part of a tour of the Aquarium, and had sat amongst the magnificent sights and smells of the blossoms at Van Dusen Gardens.

A week hence they congregated for their annual outing at Stanley Park. Some competed in the pitch-n-putt golf tournament, while others participated in lawn bowling matches.

For the week following that, they had booked tickets on the Royal Hudson's scenic ride along the Squamish Highway. The view of Howe Sound was peaceful and a few of them were talking about trying the option of returning on the ship, S.S. Britannia.

Their excursion this week had already proven a delight. While the air was chilly beside Chilliwack Lake, the beauty of the surrounding mountains more than made up for the discomfort. Hot tea brewed over the picnic firepit was also a welcome consolation.

On the way down from the lake, they insisted that the driver stop so they could watch some kayakers running the rapids above the bridge. The youthful attitude of the oldsters manifested itself in their explosions of applause and cheers as each daredevil successfully manoeuvered the boiling water.

A few of them recollected paddlers of a different nature seen in the area the previous year. The Rosedale Canoe Race was held just north of Chilliwack, and an entire flotilla of clowns, somewhat tipsy from their endeavor, had zig-zagged by on the meandering stream.

Next, they were off to Minter Gardens. This manicured oasis in the middle of the rugged mountain valley was a real treat. Azaleas, rhododendrons and tulips of all shades and colors were in season. Honeysuckle and jasmine provided the perfume. They were fascinated by the way the gardeners had sculptured intriguing shapes from shrubs. They lunched among the flowers.

The afternoon was to be spent in an area that was said to rival Switzerland. Ryder Lake, a tiny rural community with no central townsite, nestled in the fold of incredibly dramatic mountains, some saddled with glaciers. Picturesque homesteads abutted wilderness. The group was to drive around the elevated valley, where lush pastures were surrounded by rail fences and where cows wore bells. In the middle of these same pastures, the occasional cherry tree, laden with blossoms, attracted hummingbirds in such great numbers that it sounded like bees at a hive.

It was spring in Greater Vancouver.

These experiences are only a small sampling from many that are available in this unique area. Natural splendor, easily accessible to any who wish to explore it, and a metropolis that will soon become an international showcase, are magnets that draw people from all over the world to visit and often to stay.

Add to these ingredients several vital communities and a hinterland that offers an array of unusual lifestyles, and an awareness of the magic that is prevalent begins to unfold.

Turn these pages and 'Touch the Magic'.

– Ken Budd

The cast is ready. **(Jericho Beach, Vancouver)**

Summer

Happiness is a great greeting. (Children's Festival, Vanier Park, Vancouver)

Worn by time, but the memories last. **(Mission)**

A taste of the good life. **(Maple Ridge)**

Green fields kissed by the sun.. **(Ladner)**

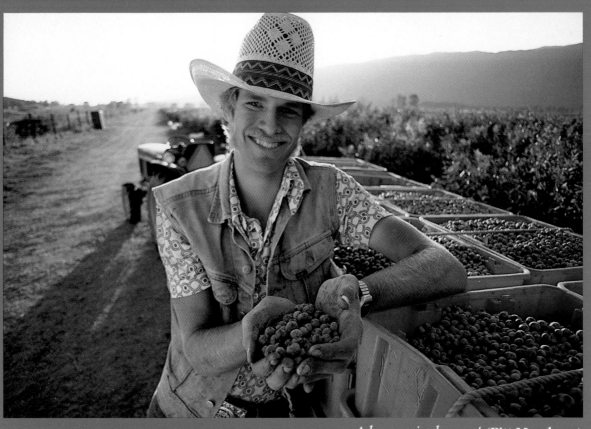

A berry nice harvest. **(Pitt Meadows)**

The smile of a survivor.

Hell and high water. (Chilliwack River)

New Canadians celebrate a special day. **(Robson Square, Vancouver)**

Marketplace meets marina. **(Granville Island Public Market, Vancouver)**

Your choice of succulence. **(Granville Island Public Market, Vancouver)**

Add sunhot raspberry to iceberg blue and you get a delicious day. **(Kitsilano Pool, Vancouver)**

A taste of the tropics.
(Bloedel Conservatory, Vancouver)

Home of the planets. **(The Planetarium, Vancouver)**

Clip-clop on cobblestones. **(Gastown, Vancouver)**

Smiles from 'Down Under'.
(Stanley Park, Vancouver)

27

The costumes of heroes vary. **(English Bay, Vancouver)**

'Hotdogging' with sails adds adventure to color. **(English Bay, Vancouver)**

Sails at anchor. (Canada Place & Coal Harbour, Vancouver)

Knights of a modern day. **(Medieval Days, Deas Island Park, Delta)**

Flagons for the bard and his maiden.
(Medieval Days, Deas Island Park, Delta)

An athletic ballet.
Asian Festival, Vanier Park, Vancouver)

A cultural feast. **(Asian Festival, Vanier Park, Vancouver)**

A lofty walkway. **(Capilano Suspension Bridge, North Shore)**

A peaceful pastime. **(Chilliwack River)**

34

This train is bound for glory! **(The Royal Hudson, Howe Sound)**

Racing for home before the plug gets pulled. **(Bathtub Race, SeaFestival, Vancouver)**

King Neptune and mate, the 'tubbers' await. **(SeaFestival, Vancouver)**

It's not the size that counts! **(Howe Sound)**

Smiling tadpoles? **(Kitsilano Pool, Vancouver)**

Fantasies in sand. **(Sandcastle Competition, White Rock**

A bird's-eye view. **(Vancouver)**

Museums and art make fascinating partners. **(Museum of Man, UBC, Vancouver)**

Spirits of song. **(Museum of Man, UBC, Vancouver)**

Zenith found. **(Surrey)**

Friends of the sky.

A centre of class and antiquity. **(Vancouver Art Gallery)**

Appreciating the works of the masters. **(Vancouver Art Gallery)**

Reflections of style. **(Vancouver)**

*And just like eagles,
they're free!*

*Wings unruffle and
stretch to tautness.*
**(Hang Gliding
Championships,
Grouse Mountain,
North Vancouver)**

48

Peaks to climb and vistas to enjoy. **(The Lions, West Vancouver)**

Hollywood North.

"Hands up!" (from 'The Grey Fox')

Blue on blue, and blue on blue. **(Kitsilano Pool, Vancouver)**

A class act. **(The Aquarium, Vancouve**

The plunge to victory. **(Aquatic Centre, Vancouver)**

Teammates trumpet support.

*Champions
commentate.*

Strokes in unison.

They're comin' around 'The Clubhouse Turn'...(**Exhibition Park, Vancouver**)

The wheels of fitness prepare to turn…

…and compete to the beat of a different hum. **(The Grand Prix, Gastown, Vancouver)**

North to Alaska. (Lions Gate Bridge, Vancouver)

Passage to adventure. **(Horseshoe Bay, West Vancouver)**

A beacon of beauty. **(Lighthouse Park, West Vancouver)**

Pax. (The Papal Visit, Abbotsford)

An afternoon's delight.
(**Spanish Banks, Vancouver**)

An international showcase celebrates coming of age. **(Sea Festival, English Bay, Vancouver)**

Nightfall mirrors special images. **(False Creek, Vancouver)**

Starkness tangos with soft pastels. **(Stanley Park, Vancouver)**

"A hunting we will go!" **(Langley)**

Lonely eyes and wet noses.

Strength, grace and 'Tally-Ho'!

The spirit of tradition.

Spontaneous mischief. **(Kitsilano, Vancouver)**

A priceless emblem. **(Lighthouse Park, West Vancouver)**

Sunbeams of beauty. (Lynn Canyon, North Vancouver)

Unique architecture flourishes. **(The Law Courts, Vancouver)**

Time to contemplate. **(Cypress Bowl, West Vancouver)**

Placid moorage. **(Point Grey, Vancouver)**

Light challenges the storm. **(North Vancouver)**

His, and…   …hers. **(Fish Hatchery, Sardis)**

Pastures blush from the touch of the early morning sun. **(Surrey)**

Crimson fingers evoke an oriental mood. **(Stanley Park, Vancouver)**

Feathers on fire. **(Stanley Park, Vancouver)**

Found a peanut. **(Stanley Park, Vancouver)**

82

Hallowe'en personified. **(Kitsilano, Vancouver)**

The heritage of the hunt. **(Maple Ridge)**

Old town meets new town. **(Gastown, Vancouver)**

Reflection on history. **(Vancouver)**

Time in a vertical tunnel. **(Vancouver)**

History in the making. **(Expo 86 Site, Vancouver)**

Smiles are infectious,... **(New Westminster)**

...and beget more smiles. **(Granville Island Public Market, Vancouver)**

Legends in tapestry.
(Museum of Man, UBC, Vancouver)

ı' south. **(Serpentine Fen, Delta)**

Customs renewed.
**(Museum of Man,
UBC, Vancouver)**

Masters of art keep legends alive...(**Museum of Man, University of British Columbia, Vancouver**)

…while games of today create new legends. **(BC Lions, B.C. Place Stadium, Vancouver)**

Grinding out the yards.

'Crazies' are part of the game.

Action on the gridiron. **(BC Lions, B.C. Place Stadium, Vancouver)**

A breather before more pain.

Shakin' great.

Mountains, mist and magic. **(Howe Sound)**

White birds must fly…(**Indian Arm, Belcarra**)

A macabre dance. (**Squamish**)

Tranquil solitude. **(Fraser River, Delta)**

We will not forget. **(Victory Square, Vancouver)**

The pride and the pain of a time past.

Canada's best pay tribute.

Winners all. **(Point Grey, Vancouver)**

Eyes of gold gather. **(Stanley Park, Vanco**

Autumn serenity. **(Vancouver)**

Ghost rider. **(Mission)**

Muck, motors and mayhem. **(Mission)**

The city floats on cotton candy. **(Vancouver)**

Workhorses of the sea glide on liquid honey. **(Fraser River, Delta)**

A new cloud is anchored to the skyline. **(B.C. Place Stadium, Vancouver)**

Mood indigo. **(Vanier Park, Vancouver)**

He shoots, but doesn't score. **(Pacific Coliseum, Vancouver)**

Hockey night in Vancouver.

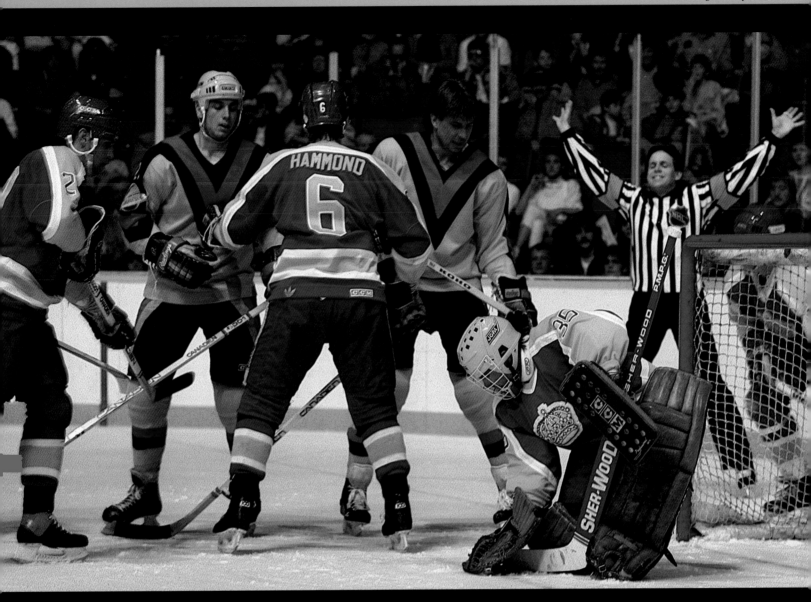

So close and yet so far.

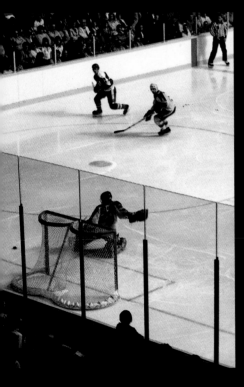

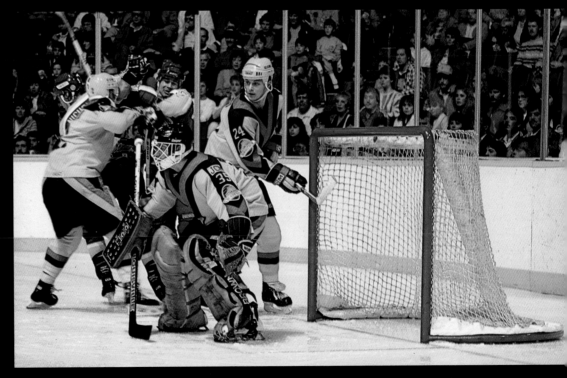

Follow the bouncing puck.

Gladiators on ice?

A haunting beginning to a new season. (Howe Sound)

A classic evening. **(Vancouver)**

A black tie affair. **(Orpheum Theatre, Vancouver)**

"The play's the thing." **(Amadeus, The Playhouse, Vancouver)**

With the deftness of butterflies… **(Queen Elizabeth Theatre, Vancouver)**

The joy of dance. **(The Nutcracker, Queen Elizabeth Theatre, Vancouver)**

Twinkling memories. **(Robson Square, Vancouver)**

A 'Downtown Christmas'.
(Robson Square, Vancouver)

Warming up to the season. **(Carol Ships, Ambleside Beach, West Vancouve**

114

The sounds of angels. **(Bentall Centre, Vancouver)**

Raising spirits.
(Bentall Centre, Vancouver)

A houseful of cheer. **(Vancouver)**

So where're the polar bears? **(Polar Bear Swim, English Bay, Vancouver)**

Refugees from Antarctica.

I would, but I just did my hair!

Here today, gone to Maui.

Big Ben has competition. **(Gastown, Vancouver)**

Wintery weather paints its own canvas. **(Kitsilano, Vancouver)**

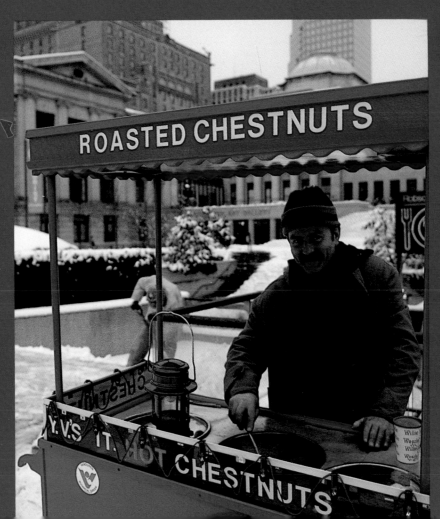

A yuletide tradition.
(Robson Square, Vancouver)

A walk on water (Boundary Bay, Delta)

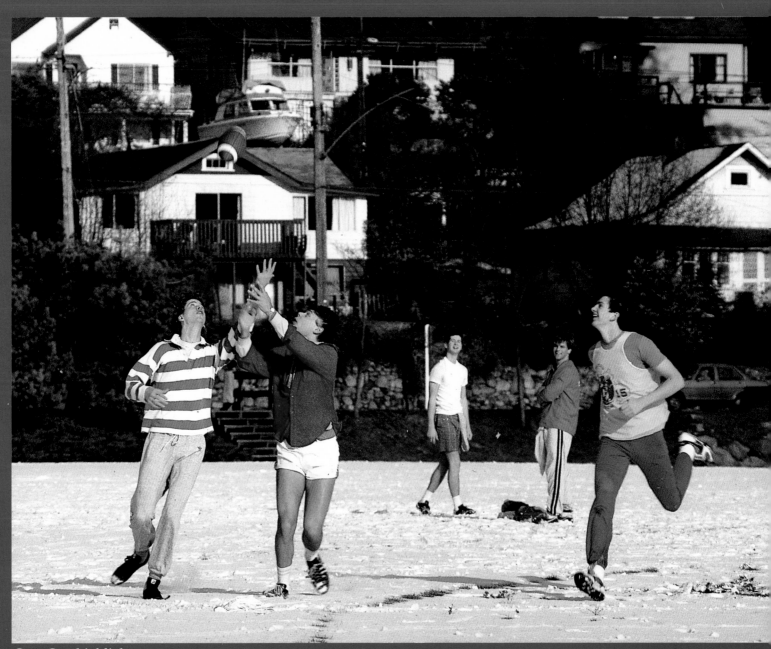

Grey Cup highlights. **(Ambleside Park, West Vancouver)**

jewelled magic. (The Grouse Nest, Grouse Mountain, North Vancouver)

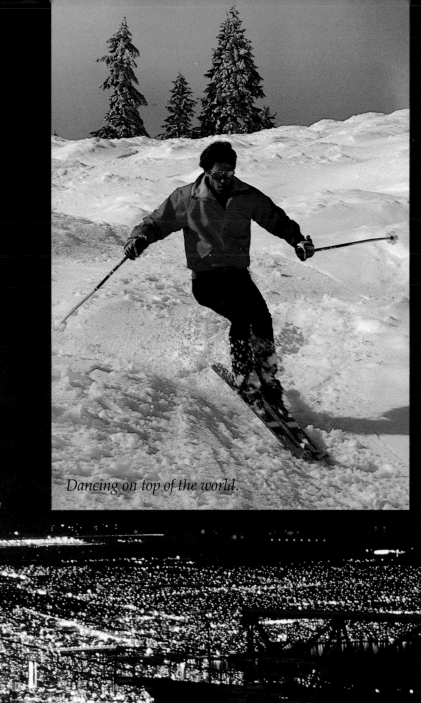

Dancing on top of the world.

Champions of tomorrow take heed. **(Whistler Mountain)**

Competitors measure the challenge. **(Whistler Mountain)**

Warmth can be found in cool places. **(Whistler Mountain)**

Harbor passage. **(SeaBus, North Vancouver)**

A rainy day pastime. **(Seabus, North Vancouver)**

Just walking in the rain. **(North Vancouver)**

Fresh snow brings a crisp winter charm. **(West End, Vancouver)**

Celebrations—beautifully bizarre.
(Chinese New Year, Chinatown, Vancouver)

An oriental smorgasbord. **(Chinatown, Vancouver)**

Boys will be boys.
**(Lady Godiva's Ride,
UBC, Vancouver)**

Sentinels stand guard. **(Mt. Seymour, North Vancouver)**

Mountain mirrors. **(Mt. Currie)**

Champions enjoy their victory.
(World Cup, Whistler)

Mountain majesty (Garibaldi Range)

Once upon a time in the west. **(Spanish Banks, Vancouver)**

The legend rides on.

Leaves of lace lighten the joggers' pace. **(Stanley Park, Vancouver)**

Spring

Nature replenishes herself. **(Stanley Park, Vancouver)**

Easter Bunny and friends.

Colorful pioneers.

Charmers.

Up, up and away. **(Hyack Festival, New Westminster)**

So who needs a cannon? **(Anvil Battery, Hyack Festival, New Westminster)**

Logging was never such fun.

Re-charging the battery.

145

Crank in that sheet!

Chariots of the wind.

Sailing on the cool and bright clear water. (Southern Straights Yacht Race, Vancouver)

'Ba, Ba Black Sheep...' **(Wool Fair, Clearbrook)**

Click go the shears, 'Boys'.

The Little Shepherd Boy.

Equine grace. **(Southlands Equestrian Centre, Vancouver)**

No tickling when tacking up.

It's a country lifestyle. **(Lanzarac Acres, Langley)**

Lore of the past train leaders.

Once in a lifetime. **(The Lions, West Vancouver)**

Peace is a priority. **(Peace March, Vancouver)**

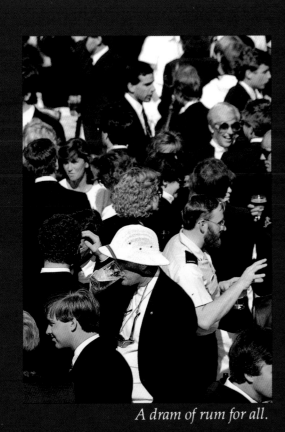

A dram of rum for all.

Sailing past.

A salute to sailing. (The Sail Past, Royal Vancouver Yacht Club, Vancouver)

Preparing for adventure. **(Aquatic Centre, Vancouver)**

Treasures of the sea. **(Howe Sound)**

Re-living traditions. **(Indian Days, Cultus Lake)**

Echoes from ancestors.

The apprentice awaits his turn. **(B.C. Rowing Championships, Burnaby Lake)**

The race is on.

Aquatic syncopation.

Rest for the toilers.

Runners unite. **(Vancouver Marathon)**

I've gotta start saving my change!" **(Vancouver)**

Why does it always rain on the parade? **(Lions Gate Bridge, Vancouver)**

Twirl your partner and promenade. **(Minter Gardens, Rosedale)**

A spring break. **(Vancouver)**

Delivering on time. **(Vancouver)**

A garden of memories. **(Nitobe Gardens, UBC, Vancouver)**

163

Just clownin' around. (Canoe Race/Rosedale)

Ready at the gate. **(Cloverdale Rodeo)**

DON'T get along little dogie!

Leather, dust and victory.

A rite of passage realized.

The pipes skirl and the procession proceeds. **(Simon Fraser University, Burnaby)**

Their journeys have given hope.
(Langley and B.C. Place Stadium)

STEVE FONYO'S
JOURNEY FOR LIVES

TRAVELAIRE

'Hands Across the Border' (Peace Arch, White Rock)

BRETHREN·DWELLING·TOGETHER·IN·UNITY

New found friends.

They run with the spirit of Mercury. **(B.C. School Track & Field Championships, Burnaby)**

Like Pegasus, they prepare to take wing.

Time to concentrate.

The way we all were. **(Vancouver)**

Sunsets become happenings. **(Kitsilano Beach, Vancouver)**

Touch the magic

Copyright © 1985 by Touch the Magic Publishing Inc.

All rights reserved. The use of any part of this
publication, reproduced, transmitted in any form or by
any means electronic, mechanical, photocopying,
recording or otherwise, or stored in a retrieval system,
without the prior consent of the publisher is an
infringement of the Copyright Law.

Published in Canada by:

Touch the Magic Publishing Inc.,
#1 155 Water Street, Gastown,
Vancouver, British Columbia, Canada.
V6B 1A7

Design: Alex Studio Limited.

CANADIAN CATALOGUING IN PUBLICATION
DATA

Hersee, Philip, 1945–
    Greater Vancouver—touch the magic

ISBN 0-9692166-0-2

1. Vancouver Metropolitan Area (B.C.) –
Description and travel – Views. I. Budd,
Ken, 1942–   II. Title.
FC3847.37.H47 1985   917.11'33   C85-091276-8
F1089.5.V22H47 1985

Colour separated, printed and bound in Hong Kong
by Scanner Art Services Inc., Toronto.